BR BLUE No 1

SOUTHAMPTON
and the
NEW FOREST

John Dedman

N.B.

© Kevin Robertson (Noodle Books) and John Dedman 2007

ISBN   (10) 0 –9554110-6-8
           (13) 978-0-9554110-6-9

First published in 2007 by Kevin Robertson
under the **NOODLE BOOKS** imprint
PO Box 279
Corhampton
SOUTHAMPTON
SO32 3ZX

www.kevinrobertsonbooks.co.uk

Printed in England by Ian Allan (Printing) Ltd.

Front cover: Push-pull fitted class 33/1 33115 heading south through the New Forest just south of Wood Fiddley with the 08.21 Leeds to Weymouth. Taken with a 250mm lens on 25th August 1983.

Preceding page: Named class 47/4 No 47535 'University of Leicester' heads north at Beaulieu Road on 15th June 1982. The loco was named a month earlier on 12th May at Leicester Station and allocated to Bescot. The train is the early morning 06.25 Poole to Liverpool inter-regional working via Birmingham.

Opposite page: On 16th February 1985 Class 47/4 47508 is heading a down inter-regional working from the Midlands, through St Denys to Bournemouth and Poole. 47508 carries the name 'Great Britain' after the iron clad steamship designed by Isambard Kingdom Brunel and built in 1843. The loco was named in March 1979, although in 1985 new plates were fitted with the name 'S.S. Great Britain'.

Rear cover: A pair of class 73/1s - 73107 and 73116 - has plenty of power in hand with only five vans forming the 4W22 11.50 Poole to Waterloo parcels. The train is passing through Hinton Admiral station on Sunday 20th January 1980.

(Note - All photographs are by the Author.)

Introduction

Railways have always been my biggest interest since I was quite young. My grandparents lived opposite the goods yard at Lymington Town station and where I would spend afternoons in the front garden watching wagons being shunted in the yard. It seemed so busy and yet when I look at the track plan now it was in fact a very small yard.

My grandfather worked for British Railways at the Pier. I remember him taking me from Town Station to Pier Station in the cab of the driving-trailer of the steam push-pull branch train. I was quite young and found the noise somewhat scary as for much of the short journey we were on the iron bridge across the river and then onto curved track accompanied by lots of wheel squealing . My father also worked for BR, but on the Lymington – Yarmouth IOW ferry. Like many others in those pre-car days, all family outings were by train, the journey starting with one and a half miles on the crossbar seat attached to Dad's bicycle as far as Lymington Town station. It was usually the 7am branch train to Brockenhurst and then across the platform for the main line London service. I remember on more than one occasion this came in behind a blue Merchant Navy pacific.

At home in pre school days during the early 50's, I had my first Tri-ang train set - the usual Jinty tank and a few wagons, later graduating to a Princess Victoria. As with the full size, model railways have been a part of my life ever since.

In 1960 I was sent to the old secondary school at Brockenhurst located next to the railway at the south end of the station. There I found I was not alone in my interest as lots of us boys spent all of our break times watching the trains.

I also got my first introduction to the Ian Allan ABC Locospotters books from which I could now both identify the trains and likewise find out more about the locos. A few months later I was given an old bicycle and which gave me the transport I needed to get closer to the railway.

From my home in Pennington it was a three mile ride to Sway, and the station of the same name on the main line to Bournemouth.

Near here were also some good vantage points from the cattle bridges of the Forest heath-lands towards Lymington Junction. This led on to a few years following trains around the south, including day trips to the various London termini. Other visits were to locations such as Salisbury, Westbury and Reading.

As the steam engines I had been brought up with started to fade away so around 1966 I lost interest and eventually moved abroad to work. When finally settled back in the area in 1973, I moved to New Milton where my new home backed on to the Bournemouth main line. Coupled with the regular passing of trains my curiosity was re-kindled. I had also graduated into an fondness for photography and accordingly trains were a natural subject. With more opportunity also to travel, my outings were not just confined to the New Forest area and up to the late 1990s I recorded the railway scene in most of the British Isles. Privatisation though has resulted in another lessening of interest for the current scene.

At the same time as the move to a more permanent home, I started building a model railway and also joined the local New Forest Model Railway Society formed in 1975. The Society is currently based at Brockenhurst Village Hall, ironically built on the site of my old school adjacent to the railway. Here we have an annual exhibition at the end of May, and also a Club Open Day at the end of November. My own modelling interests cover a wide range from the 1960's through to the 1980's and in both OO and O gauges. I have also been involved with exhibiting layouts at shows across the country for over two decades, one of my layouts, 'Hollybank Depot', featuring in the 'Model Rail supplement of 'Rail' magazine.

Book Content

This collection of photographs were all taken on the lines through Southampton and the New Forest between 1975 and 1985.

Carefully selected from my collection of 35mm colour slides and negatives, I have tried to illustrate both the everyday trains and some of the more unusual workings. Time though marches on, and whilst to some the collection may appear 'modern' none of these scenes with this type of train are around today. As well as spending time finding vantage points, an equal amount of time was spent waiting for some of the less common train workings, particularly as freight and boat trains do not always turn up on schedule. Likewise as will also be seen in the views, it is not just the trains that have disappeared, the backgrounds, signal boxes, signals and even the station colour schemes, all are now different.

The main line through to Bournemouth has always been a busy route with the backbone of the through passenger services in the hands of Electric Multiple Units. Diesel Electric Multiple Units were used on the cross country trains from Portsmouth to Salisbury. The longer Portsmouth to Bristol and Cardiff cross country services hauled by Class 31 and 33 diesels during this period. Diesel locos of Classes 33 and 47 were also seen on a regular basis on the Inter-Regional passenger workings as well as freight and parcels duties. More variety came from the Class 73 Electro-diesels on services which used the electrified London main line, but were restricted usually to parcels, freight and boat trains. Finally the Class 56 diesel locomotives arrived from Westbury on the Totton stone wagons. The only contemporary type missing were the Class 74 Electro-diesels, these being phased out at this time - even so I have included this type on their last workings.

Southampton itself has always had a good variety of train types and because of this I would visit regularly to photograph the cross country workings. Boat trains in and out of the Docks were another draw as well as the freight services, some of which did not travel west of Southampton.

During 1984 and 1985 the tunnel at Southampton had extensive repairs carried out with the track reduced to a single line. This meant that all freight trains from the west side of the River Test had to reverse at Redbridge, and then travel via Nursling and Romsey to use the re-instated Laverstock loop at Salisbury and so regain the main line towards London. Freightliner trains from both Southampton Freightliner Terminals (Millbrook and Maritime) also departed west to take this route, and likewise access London or the line north via Reading. Whilst such a restriction at Southampton was no doubt a headache to the operators, it did afford a lot more opportunities to photograph freight - some of which are included in this volume.

I mentioned earlier the time taken walking through various parts of the New Forest to different locations on the railway looking for suitable vantage points. Sometimes these trips formed the basis of a family outing accompanied by my wife and two young sons. Fortunately the boys were always keen to watch the trains. My wife was not forgotten either as she maintains an interest in the forest flora, fauna and wildlife.

During steam days it was noticeable that embankments and cuttings were deliberately kept free of vegetation to reduce the fire risk. Even so I recall there being regular lineside fires especially in late summer. These same locations were still relatively growth free during the early 1970's and in consequence provided for excellent views of the railway. However since that time nature has reclaimed what was rightly hers and today nearly all of these same vantage points have disappeared behind dense growth of elder, scrub and silver birch.

For my earlier photos I used a Pentax Spotmatic 35mm camera with both standard and 200mm lenses. From 1979 onwards I changed to a Canon 'A' series using varying lenses from 35 to 300mm. For railway work my favourite has always been an 85mm F1.8 and which I believe gives good perspective as well as plenty of speed with its large aperture. The earlier photos were taken on Kodachrome 64, whilst for dull weather Ektachrome slide film was used due to its associated faster shutter speed. Other film types have included Agfa CT18 and Fuji 100, although since the introduction of Kodachrome 200 this has been my main slide film. A small number of the views were taken on Kodak Gold negative film.

I would like to dedicate this book to my wife Janet for all her support when taking the photos and also help with the preparation of this volume. It is hoped that future volumes in the 'BR Blue' series will include – Western Region, Freight in the Blue-era,
Electric Locos, and The Midlands, although not necessarily in that order!

John Dedman.
Brockenhurst - 2007

47375 heading north towards St Denys station with the 6M23 10.12 Fawley to Longport Junction 100 ton bogie LPG tanks on 2nd October 1984. The orange line around the tanks denotes that they are pressurised to keep the gas in a liquid form. Longport is in the potteries area of Stoke-on-Trent and the LPG is used for firing the kilns.

Right: A wintry scene at Bevois Park Sidings on Saturday 9th February 1985. 73132 in large logo blue livery is just about to depart with the 6Y80 09.46 Southampton Up yard to Halling R.P.C. Rugby Cement wagons. At this time there were two rail-served cement terminals at this yard, Tunnel and Rugby, with an additional Blue Circle cement terminal being located in nearby Northam Yard.

Below: 45041 passing south through St Denys station with the 6V83 16.25 Eastleigh East Yard to Severn Tunnel Junction Speedlink mixed freight train on 11th October 1985. Class 45's were unusual in the Southampton area, but during 1985 they shared this working with class 47 and class 56 locos. The engine had arrived on the 6O42 08.30 from Severn Tunnel Junction due at Eastleigh at 13.25. 45041 was originally named 'The Royal Tank Regiment' but had lost it's nameplates by 1985.

On 29th March 1985 33022 is departing from Southampton Up Yard with a rake of Tunnel Cement vacuum braked Pressflo wagons. This was the Monday, Wednesday and Friday only 7M40 17.44 service to Tring Cutting. Behind the wagons can be seen two more freight trains waiting for their respective locos to arrive, a mixed rake of air braked wagons forming a later Speedlink working and a trainload of Ford vehicles from the Eastleigh factory. On the skyline is the location of the then TVS television studio, gasometers which are now the site of St Mary's football stadium, the Blue Circle cement silo, and the orange silo of Rugby Cement.

The 1O86 13.40 Exeter to Brighton Saturday only through train recorded at Mount Pleasant crossing on 29th August 1981. This service was normally hauled by two class 33s during the summer due to extra coaches being added. In charge are 33037 and 33046. The train included a RMB buffet car in its formation of 12 Mark 1 vehicles. In the background can be seen Northam Yard, and the Total 100 ton bogie tanks which arrived earlier in the day from Langley in West London. These will later form the Monday 6B67 departure to the Esso refinery at Fawley

With the River Itchen in the background, unit 1401 passes under clear signals as it approaches Mount Pleasant crossing with the 16.25 Portsmouth to Southampton local on 29th August 1981. This set was formed into a 3-car unit in 1979 at Eastleigh Works, using vehicles from 2-car Class 204 2H unit 1121 with an ex EPB driving trailer 2nd in the centre. The centre car was previously used in a disbanded class 206 3R Reading to Redhill 'Tadpole' unit.

Right: 4TC unit number 405, crossing Canute Road from the Eastern Docks - the leading set of two similar units being propelled by a class 73 electro-diesel. The train is a Boat Train to Waterloo with passengers from the P&O cruise liner 'Sea Princess'. Saturday 11th September 1982.

Lower: 73002 has just crossed Canute road with empty stock from a 'Queen Elizabeth 2' Boat Train on 28th August 1982. This will have just unloaded its passengers in the Eastern Docks and is now heading back to London – probably Clapham Junction. On the right are the former curved platforms of the derelict Southampton Terminus station. To the left is the former Goods Depot still in use today but now as a car park site for the City University. Since this view was taken the former Platforms 1 and 2 have been demolished and this area too is used for car parking. 73002 is of class 73/0 and was one of the first batch of six class 73 electro-diesels to be built originally numbered E6001 to E6006.

Above: 33013 is approaching Chapel Road Crossing with an Ocean Liner Boat Train from Waterloo to Southampton Eastern Docks, Friday 22nd April 1983. The train is carrying passengers for the Cunard liner 'Queen Elizabeth 2' which was due to depart on a cruise in the early evening. Notice the loco is fitted with miniature snow ploughs whilst the train is a dedicated set of Mk1 and Mk2 coaches used mainly for these Boat Trains between Waterloo and Southampton Docks

Right: The diverted 14.38 Waterloo to Exeter passenger train having just left the tunnel and approaching the station at Southampton on 9th March 1985. The loco is class 50 50047 'Swiftsure' named in 1978 after a former WW2 Royal Navy Cruiser. (The same name was previously carried by LMS Jubilee engine No 5716.) The train had been diverted via Southampton due to weekend engineering work on its normal route between Basingstoke and Salisbury. In addition it has run wrong line through the tunnel due to the single line working because of local engineering work.

Right: A view of the tracks between Southampton Central station and the tunnel mouth on 9th March 1985. At this time there was repair work being carried out inside the tunnel and the main line was reduced to single line working. The rails of the works narrow gauge railway can be seen on both sides of the main line. The train is the 14.40 Poole to Liverpool Lime Street hauled by a class 47/4. During this period of work most freight trains to and from the west side of Southampton were diverted via the reinstated Laverstock loop at Salisbury. This included freightliners for the Millbrook and Maritime terminals, and also the Speedlink services of oil, steel and stone to Marchwood, Fawley, Wytch Farm, Hamworthy and Totton.

Above: 47407 has just emerged from the tunnel under the city centre and is about to enter Southampton station on 9th March 1985. The train is the 08.05 from Newcastle to Poole made up mainly of clean Mk2 air conditioned coaches but spoilt by the weathered BG behind the loco. The loco is 'Aycliffe' after Newton Aycliffe in County Durham where it was named in late 1984. The engine also carries an unusual livery with the yellow of the front end extending over the cab roof.

Right: 4TC unit No 414 leading a Waterloo to Weymouth train at Southampton Central in June 1976. This is the only stop of the fast service between Waterloo and Bournemouth. At the latter station the first four coaches are detached to be taken forward to Weymouth as a stopping train by a class 33/1 diesel. On the left is the headcode '93' 4 VEP unit which will follow as an all-stations stopper to Bournemouth.

12

Above: The full gantry recorded on a cold morning. The signal box controlling the array is out of camera to the right. The actual box still stands today although now long used for other purposes with signalling in the area under remote operation from Eastleigh. There had been rumours that the actual gantry was to be taken down and sympathetically re-erected at the National Railway Museum as one of the last reasonable size arrays of semaphore signal remaining. Unfortunately this did not happen.

Left: Viewed through the signal gantry at Southampton Central a Hampshire 3H 3-car diesel electric multiple unit No 1102 approaches the station with a Salisbury to Portsmouth Harbour local passenger service in September 1980. The cranes of the Eastern Docks can be seen in the background.

Class 47 No 47351 passes a group of young spotters as it crawls through platform 3 at Southampton Central with a well loaded Freightliner train in September 1980. This was the 4O79 08.50 Ripple Lane to Southampton Maritime Saturday working.

Top: Class 73/1 73135 with the 1W95 20.08 Waterloo to Weymouth Quay Boat Train in Platform 4 at Southampton Central, 21.30 on the evening of 28th June 1980. The passengers would subsequently arrive on Weymouth Quay at 23.20 ready for the overnight ship to the Channel Islands.

Lower: 4VEP unit No 7851 waits at Southampton on the evening of 28th June 1980. The headcode '93' is for the 19.42 Waterloo to Bournemouth stopping train which was scheduled to spend 15 minutes here, during which time the 20.35 Waterloo to Weymouth fast train will precede it.

Class 31/4 31420 with 10.07 Portsmouth Harbour to Cardiff at Southampton, 8th April 1980. Loco hauled stock with Class 31/1s replaced SR and WR diesel multiple units on these services in May 1977 and they were subsequently taken over by 31/4s fitted with electric train heating the following October. The centre BG in what was a five vehicle rake was positioned as such due to short length platforms at some of the country stations.

Class 31/4 31401 with the 08.20 Cardiff to Portsmouth at Southampton on 8th April 1980. After less than three years working these trains the end was already near for these locos on the cross country services and they were replaced by Class 33s in May 1980.

On 16th February 1985 33119 leaves Southampton Central station with a lightweight parcels service composed of just one Mk1 BG. It has departed from the down bay, Platform 5, and is heading for the Western Docks.

Class 47 No 47250 with the 6V31 10.40 Totton to Westbury ARC empty PGA stone hoppers approaching Southampton Central station on 8th April 1980. This service will take the single track route from Eastleigh through Chandlers Ford to Romsey and thence on to Westbury. From that location it will then work back to the ARC quarry at Whatley in Somerset for reloading with stone.

Above: 73142 'Broadlands' at the head of the Royal Train and approaching Millbrook on 4th August 1983. The loco was named on 25th September 1980 at Romsey station by Lord Romsey. It is seen here heading for the Western Docks which it will access at the junction just beyond Millbrook station.

Opposite top: Named Class 33 33027 leaves Southampton with the 10.10 Portsmouth Harbour to Bristol cross country train on 16th February 1985. 33027 was named 'Earl Mountbatten of Burma' in September 1980 after it had been involved with hauling the late Earl's funeral train.

Opposite lower: A busy scene at the western approaches to Southampton Central station, 16th February 1985. Nearest the camera 47318 with empty Cartic wagons is held at signals on the up slow line. Beyond this another member of the class, 47606 has just left the station with empty stock from the 08.58 from Manchester Piccadilly. Here it making its way into the up loop where the loco will run-round ready for a return working north later in the afternoon. 47606 was originally numbered D1666 and in 1965 carried the name 'ODIN' - the first of the class to be named. Subsequently it was renumbered 47081 before becoming 47606 in 1983. The name was carried for 25 years until 1990, possibly the longest period a class 47 carried the same name. Finally 33119 is running light engine to the down bay platform ready to pick up a parcels train.

Class 33/1 33107 has just left the Western Docks with passengers from the P&O cruise ship 'Sea Princess' on Saturday 7th August 1982 . It is seen passing Millbrook signal box, whilst in the background is the Millbrook Freightliner container terminal that was built on the site of the former station goods yard. The carriages are a typical formation for an ocean liner service and consist of a GUV van, five Mk2 Corridor firsts, a Mk1 Brake composite, four Mk1 Open seconds and another Brake composite. The cruise ships would normally dock about 7am and the train was scheduled to depart around 10am. It would return from Waterloo about 5pm with the passengers for the next cruise due to set sail around 7pm.

Two class 73 Electro-diesels 73135 and 73131 double head the 1W96 15.30 Weymouth Quay to Waterloo Channel Island Boat Train on 15th August 1981. The stock has just crossed the River Test and is just about to pass Redbridge signal box and station: arrival in London will be at 18.50. The tracks on the left are part of the Redbridge Engineers' Yard.

08892 with an engineers wagon at the rear of Redbridge station on 25th July 1984. The track off to the right leads into the C.C.E. works yard where track sections and points were assembled. This yard was quite extensive with around 20 sidings and facilities which included a rail welding plant, creosote plant, stores, machine shop, sawmill, loading docks and a wharf on the River Test estuary.

LIMIT
OF
SHUNT

Above: Class 47 47286 arriving at Redbridge with vacuum braked steel wagons on 25th July 1984. This train has come from South Wales and the loco will run round the wagons before continuing down through the New Forest to Hamworthy where they will be loaded with imported steel coil. Imported steel at Hamworthy includes steel billott for Cardiff Rod Mill, steel coil for Austin Rover (Pressed Steel Fisher) at Swindon and steel coil for Round Oak. The British Rail Leyland Sherpa van is in the Redbridge Engineers' Yard.

Left: Running wrong line so it can access the yard at Redbridge is 47299, with the 6H60 07.20 Salisbury to Marchwood air-braked trip freight, 4th September 1984. The class 47 loco will run round its wagons in the yard and then depart across the river Test and through Totton to the Fawley branch. The wagons are all carrying military vehicles and are destined for the M.O.D. base at Marchwood.

Above: 47053 has just crossed the River Test and is about to enter the yard at Redbridge with CV94, the Wednesday only 10.00 cement train Hamworthy BCI to Rhoose in South Wales, 25th July 1984. Here it will run round and then depart on the line to the right to Salisbury via Nursling.

Left: A class 205 3-car Hampshire unit No 1124 in plain blue livery skirts the River Test as it takes the Romsey line at Redbridge with a local stopping train to Salisbury in October 1980. Redbridge station can be seen on the extreme right. The two carmine and cream Mk1 coaches behind the train belonged to a private organisation and carry the name 'Solent Rigging (Services) Limited' on the roof boards.

Above: Class 205 3-car Hampshire Unit No 1130 with a Southampton to Salisbury local train near the site of the former Nursling station on 15th August 1981. These sets were built at Eastleigh in 1957 and at first carried the then standard green livery for coaching stock. In the late sixties they were repainted plain blue although a number subsequently carried the later blue/grey passenger coach livery.

Right: Class 50 No 50005 approaching Redbridge with the diverted 12.20 Exeter to Waterloo on 9th March 1985. 50005 was named 'Collingwood' after the World War One battleship. The loco has been refurbished and carries the blue large logo livery. The Class 50 locos had a top speed of 100mph and took over the Waterloo to Exeter trains from Class 33s in May 1980.

73142 'Broadlands' with the Prince and Princess of Wales on board, being transported to Broadlands near Romsey after the Royal Wedding. The train was a special formation and consisted of Mk2 FK S13401, Mk1 BCK 21268 and the Southern Region General Manager's saloon TDB975025. The loco carries a unique headcode of CD for the special occasion and is heading north through Nursling on 28th July 1981.

33113 heading past the lower Test marshes nature reserve towards Nursling on 29th April 1983. The train is the Fridays only 6E25 15.45 Fawley to Purfleet bitumen tank units and has just left Redbridge where it ran round its stock after arriving from the Fawley branch. Like many other freight trains during 1983 and 1984 it is taking this route so as to avoid the engineering work being carried out in Southampton tunnel where single line working was in operation.

47148 heads containers south over the crossing at Nursling with the 4O82 02.00 Coatbridge to Millbrook Freightliner depot, 26th August 1983.

Above: A pair of class 33s - 33005 and 33044 - has just passed under the M27 motorway bridge with a heavily loaded container train on 27th July 1984. This was the 4O81 03.00 Coatbridge to Southampton Maritime Freightliner Terminal and where it is due to arrive at 15.34, after a 12 hour journey from Glasgow.

Right: On 29th August 1981 a pair of class 31s, 31247 and 31145 are approaching Nursling with the 09.10 Swansea to Portsmouth Harbour summer Saturday passenger train. The return working was at 14.10 from Portsmouth Harbour and destined for Cardiff Central. Double heading was used on summer Saturdays as the load was increased to ten vehicles compared to the usual six on weekdays.

47267 heads north at Nursling with the 6V37 Furzebrook Oil Sidings to Llandarcy oil tanks, 26th August 1983. The train is made up of BP 100 ton bogie oil tanks carrying crude oil from the Wytch Farm oil wells in Dorset to the Llandarcy refinery in South Wales. These trains ceased running when a pipeline was installed from Wytch Farm to the BP oil terminal at Hamble.

47053 with the 6V94 10.00 Hamworthy to Rhoose (South Wales) block cement train. This was a Wednesdays-only working and was another service which reversed at Redbridge to take the Salisbury line. It was photographed heading north at Nursling on 25th July 1984.

A work-stained 56043 at Nursling on 25th July 1984 with the 6V31 10.40 Totton ARC to Westbury stone empties. The train was unloaded in the yard on the Eling tramway which is a short branch less than half a mile from Totton yard. This meant that the loco had to run round its wagons at both Totton and Redbridge yards. 56043 was then allocated to Bristol Bath Road Depot but was working out of Westbury at the time.

3H unit No 1133 heading for Salisbury with a train from Portsmouth, recorded at Nursling on 9th February 1985.

An unidentified 3H crosses the snow covered landscape at Nursling with a Salisbury to Southampton local, 9th February 1985.

As the boys play on the ice, the driver of a 3H diesel unit gives a toot as he passes with a local passenger train from Salisbury to Southampton, 16th February 1985.

33025 'Sultan' crossing the River Test at high tide westwards towards Totton on 14th May 1983 with the down 'Beaulieu Belle' using the VSOE 'Orient Express' Pullman Coaches. This train ran on a semi-regular basis on certain Saturdays during the summer months and terminated at Brockenhurst. From here the passengers were taken by road to the National Motor Museum at Beaulieu. The loco was named 'Sultan' on 6th August 1981 at Portsmouth Harbour station.

4 REP unit No 3005 heads a headcode '92' service through Totton on 23rd August 1980. This is a Bournemouth to Waterloo semi-fast train with intermediate stops at the more important stations on the route. On the left and beyond the signal is the start of the Eling tramway branch.

A class 47/4 passes Totton yard on Saturday 10th November 1984 with the 08.58 Manchester Piccadilly to Bournemouth inter-regional passenger train. On the right is a rake of empty tank wagons which will be collected on Monday morning to form the 7B65 08.22 from Totton to Esso Fawley ready for loading at the refinery. The vehicles themselves are vacuum braked TSV 35ton bitumen tanks, but which were soon to be converted to air brakes over the next two years and re-coded as TSA.

33023 with the 6B63 11.35 Eastleigh to Fawley Speedlink trip working at Marchwood on 4th July 1986. The train would arrive at Fawley at 12.35 and drop off the empty tanks. The engine would then depart again at 13.15 at the head of a rake of loaded tanks.

33023 with the 6B72 Fawley to Eastleigh Speedlink trip working at Marchwood on 4th July 1986. The signal is for the passing loop at this long closed station. After arrival at Eastleigh the loaded tanks would be re-marshalled into overnight Speedlink mixed freight trains to various parts of the country. Marchwood still retains its mechanical signalling twenty years later and likewise remains the only crossing point for freight traffic on the Fawley branch.

47297 at Hounsdown on the single track Fawley branch with the 6O52 08.10 Southampton Down Yard to Fawley, 4th September 1984. The wagons are 35 ton TSV bitumen tanks which arrived at Southampton in the early hours of the morning on their way to Fawley for reloading. The 47 has recently been fitted with a high intensity headlight but this has yet to be painted yellow. Unusually also the loco carries its number on the cab front where the light has been fitted.

Above: Class 33/0 33022 complete with miniature snowploughs near Lyndhurst Road on 22nd March 1983. The engine is working the 6W70 11.13 Furzebrook Clay Sidings to Eastleigh Speedlink trip working; the air braked wagon types include OCA, VEA and VDA vehicles. This photograph was taken with an 85mm lens.

Left: 33023 with the 6B72 Fawley to Eastleigh Speedlink trip service passing through the cutting at Hythe on 27th June 1986. The wagons are 45 ton 4-wheel tank wagons carrying gas oil and destined for distribution to various BR diesel depots across the south.

4 REP unit No 3008 leading the 07.55 Bournemouth to Waterloo semi-fast service through Lyndhurst Road station on 8th March 1982. The buffet and kitchen are in the third coach. On these services when meals were being served a section of the fourth coach was given over for use as a restaurant car. This station has since been appropriately renamed Ashurst (New Forest) a far more appropriate name for the local community as by road it is over two miles from Lyndhurst.

2 HAP unit No 6094 forms the 2B22 07.57 Lymington Pier to Eastleigh through train. This was the only through train from the Lymington branch on weekdays with all others terminating at Brockenhurst. It is seen approaching Lyndhurst Road on 8th March 1982.

With 1550hp available, class 33/1 33113 has plenty of power for the morning vacuum braked fitted freight from Eastleigh to Poole and Furzebrook. The train consists of a single VVV van and four MCV mineral wagons and has just passed through Lyndhurst Road station running into the heart of the New Forest on a frosty 8th March 1982.

Above: 4 VEP unit number 7711 approaching Lyndhurst Road station in the New Forest with the Sunday Lymington Pier to Eastleigh on 13th February 1983. The headcode on the front of this train is reversed and should read 97 and not 79.

Right: On 22nd March 1983 4 VEP unit 7813 has just left Lyndhurst Road station on a down stopping service.

Above: 33105 heading south through the forest towards Beaulieu Road on 15th June 1982. The wagons are 45 ton oil tanks, possibly carrying fuel oil for vessels at Weymouth Quay.

Right: 47552 heads south across an open area of forest towards Beaulieu Road station with an inter-regional passenger train on Tuesday 29th May 1984. The location is one of the many New Forest animal underpass bridges provided to give ponies and cattle freedom to roam the forest.

Left: Retimed to depart one minute later for the summer timetable, 2 HAP unit No 6091 forms the 07.58 Lymington Pier to Eastleigh on the morning of 15th June 1982. The unit is passing through the cutting just north of Beaulieu Road station but will soon be in open forest again.

Right: On the evening of 5th July 1979 Class 73 73106 is just south of Beaulieu Road station with the 4B21 down parcels vans, the 16.53 Eastleigh to Bournemouth. On this occasion it was formed of just a plain blue ex LMS BG and a blue/grey BR Mk1 BG.

Lower: Class 33/1 33107 seen on 26th August 1983 climbing towards Beaulieu Road station with the 7W56 11.13 Furzebrook Clay sidings to Eastleigh East Yard freight. 33107 was one of a small number of class 33s which had their window surrounds painted white at this time. The train is vacuum braked and made up of both steel-carrying wagons and mineral wagons.

A push pull fitted Class 33/1 hauling a short air braked freight consisting of two OCA and three OBA open wagons forming the 6W70 11.13 Furzebrook Clay sidings to Eastleigh East Yard . The train is approaching Wood Fiddley on 25th August 1983. The Speedlink air braked freight network had been introduced in 1977 but it was a few years before it reached this area.

47121 approaching Wood Fiddley with the 6V37 12.55 Furzebrook Oil Sidings to Llandarcy tanks on 22nd August 1983, comprised of ten 100 ton bogie tanks.

Right: Class 47/4 47444 'University of Nottingham' heading north through the forest at Wood Fiddley with the 17.05 Poole to Derby on 21st May 1983. The loco was named at Nottingham Station in May 1981 to mark the centenary of the University.

Below: On Saturday 3rd June 1978, 47460 is heading south from Beaulieu Road to Weymouth with the 06.54 from Halifax. In the previous April this loco was fitted with the unofficial name of 'Great Eastern' at Stratford Depot in east London but the nameplate had been removed by this time. The light grey roof of the loco was a trade mark of Stratford engines.

33002 and 33003 heading across Bishop's Dyke towards Beaulieu Road station with 6V94 18.32 Poole to Westbury Blue Circle cement Pressflos. This train ran on Tuesday and Thursday evenings and was usually double headed, 5th July 1979.

Class 47 47508 'Great Britain' climbs across Bishop's Dyke with the 4B26 19.44 Bournemouth to Waterloo up evening parcels vans on 5th July 1979.

On 30th July 1983 47101 is seen across the fields from Brockenhurst at the head of the Saturday 12.40 Poole to Manchester. Twenty years earlier this train would have carried the 'Pines Express' name.

A 4 REP unit leading the 06.55 Bournemouth to Waterloo train away from Brockenhurst on a frosty 11th April 1980. Breakfast will be served in the fourth coach, the white menus for which can just be seen through the windows.

A 2 SAP unit on the approach to Brockenhurst with the 06.45 Eastleigh to Lymington Pier on 11th April 1980. These 2 car units were originally built in 1957 as 2 HAP units with some were converted in 1974 to all second class and the revised 2 SAP designation.

On 10th July 1976 Class 47 47218 is approaching Brockenhurst with a down Inter-regional passenger train from the Midlands. The loco still has its route indicator blinds fitted although the former reporting codes are no longer displayed.

Top: 33118 + 73111 with the 4W22 11.50 Poole to Waterloo parcels 17th February 1980, this train was often double headed, but more usually by a pair of class 73s. The service is just east of Brockenhurst the station and level crossing just visible in the background.

Lower: Class 73 73123 at Brockenhurst with 4B21, the down evening parcels vans formed of a BR GUV and an ex LMS BG both in plain BR blue livery. 4B21 was the 16.53 Eastleigh to Bournemouth and it is running wrong line over the level crossing to access platform 1 in the station after using the crossover. The very decorative building behind the loco is the original crossing keeper's cottage, its function was replaced by the East or 'A' signal box later built in front of it. 'A' signal box was itself later removed and replaced by the current signal box on the opposite side of the main line. 20th July 1979

The Class 74 farewell tour special running into platform 3 at Brockenhurst, 3rd December 1977. 74003 has a nine coach train made up of two 4TC sets with a buffet car in the centre. After leaving Brockenhurst the special traversed the Lymington branch and also visited Romsey and Southampton Docks. The service was organised jointly by Railway Pictorial and Publications, and the Diesel and Electric Group.

Miniature snow plough fitted 33013 approaches platform 1 at Brockenhurst with the 'Beaulieu Belle' on 27th August 1983. On this occasion platform 1 was being used as platform 4, on the down side, was in regular use by the Lymington branch train. This also meant the need for running wrong line over the level crossing. Having disgorged its passengers for the road trip to Beaulieu the empty stock was taken to Bournemouth until required for the return working to London at the end of the afternoon.

In May 1978 a pair of class 33s head north through Brockenhurst station with an engineers train carrying track panels. Brockenhurst 'B' signal box can be seen on the right with the down starting signals for platforms 3 and 4 on the left. The headcode is somewhat appropriate from a personal perspective.

Top: The Brockenhurst to Stirling Motorail train at Brockenhurst on 8th June 1980. This overnight service arrived from Stirling at 06.30 on Saturday and 07.30 on Sunday mornings at Brockenhurst. The return service departed Saturday and Sunday evenings. The train consisted of two sleeping cars, a corridor first, a corridor brake first and the car flats. Following departure the train was attached to a similar service from Dover - usually in west London, and then the combined service formed a 20 vehicle long train for the overnight journey north to Stirling via the west coast main line. This was hauled by an a.c. electric loco.

Right: An earlier view of the same service recorded in May 1977 at Brockenhurst and showing part of the Motorail train with a class 33 loco and Mk1 second class sleeping car. In the background are the few sidings that remain in the goods yard.

A headcode 93 all stations stopping train passing Lymington Junction on its journey from Bournemouth to Waterloo. It is formed of 4 VEP unit numbered 7821 on 7th May 1980. The Lymington branch line can be seen in the foreground and curving away to the left. This was also the site for the junction of the 'old road' to Bournemouth via Ringwood and Wimborne and which curved off to the right at the rear of the train.

4 VEP unit number 7715 with the Sunday 08.55 Eastleigh to Lymington Pier heading south across the forest heath at Setley on the Lymington branch, 10th February 1980.

Right: 4VEP unit No 7704 arriving at Lymington Pier with the 11.40 from Brockenhurst on 28th December 1979. The Freshwater car and passenger ferry is moored on the left side of the slipway.

Lower: With moored fishing boats in the foreground 2 Hap unit No 6034 is just about to cross the Lymington River with the 13.57 from the Pier to Brockenhurst on 9th April 1980. The Railway Bridge across the river links the Town and Pier stations and being such a low bridge is the northern limit of navigation for most boats sailing up river.

74004 on the 1W17 09.36 Waterloo to Weymouth Quay Channel Island Boat Train after passing Lymington Junction on 10th July 1976. This was a summer service which ran until early October.

One of the last vacuum braked mixed freight trains climbing away from Brockenhurst. 6W61, the 06.58 Eastleigh East Yard to Poole hauled by 33015 on 11th April 1980.

During May in 1978 the down line between Brockenhurst and Sway is in the process of being re-ballasted. The loco is 33032 crawling along as the ballast is being dropped on to the track from the bogie Seacow wagons.

Two-Car Departmental De-Icing and service unit No 001 heading down the main line from New Milton on 28th June 1979. This unit was made up of two converted motor coaches from former 2 HAL units in 1967.

73123 + 73131 approaching New Milton on Monday 5th May 1980 with the 5W44 09.40 Weymouth to Clapham Junction ECS Vans.

After an overnight snowfall in February 1978 there are no electric trains running at New Milton. Instead a substitute diesel service provides a poor substitute and comprising two Hampshire units not normally seen on this service, 3H unit 1124 and 2H unit 1129.

A year later on 2nd January 1979 and after another snowfall at New Milton, the 11.00 Bournemouth to Waterloo semi-fast is formed of 33116 pushing two 4TC units. Services were very disrupted due to ice and snow on the third rail, and the diesel was in place of the normal 4 REP unit used to power the train. The leading TC unit is No 428.

47226 is working hard up the gradient with its eight coach load as it approaches Hinton Admiral station on 7th July 1979. This was the summer Saturday 1M02 08.42 Poole to Liverpool Lime Street which only ran until 29th September.

Acknowledgements – Railway Magazine 1975 to 1985, Modern Railways Magazine 1977 to 1981, Ian Allan Motive Power ABC's, and John Fox for access to his collection of timetables.